Daedal Doodle

Victor Stabin

VICTOR
STABIN

This book is dedicated to my parents, who exposed me to the extraordinary, with extra special thanks to Skyler and Arielle Stabin.

Text and illustration ©2011 Victor Stabin
Published by Victor Stabin Books

Illustrated by Victor Stabin   Layout and Design by Andrij Borys Associates

First Edition
Printed in Mexico

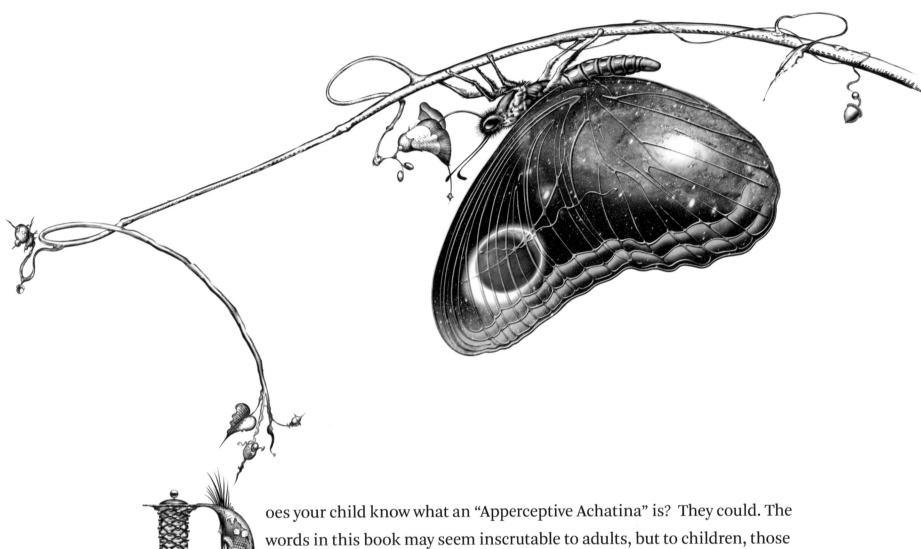

Does your child know what an "Apperceptive Achatina" is? They could. The words in this book may seem inscrutable to adults, but to children, those natural language sponges, they are simply some new words to absorb. Children just want you to turn the page so they can see the next drawing.

Daedal, this book's namesake is defined as "ingeniously formed or working, skillful and artistic." The word's origin comes from the mythic, Greek architect, inventor and craftsman Daedalus. The magic is in the *Doodle*.

These alliterative words and characters are the product of 8,000 pages of dictionary reading distilled into an ABC book for the curious of all ages. My five-year-old child now knows what an "epizoon" is. Do you?

"Daddy, turn the page."

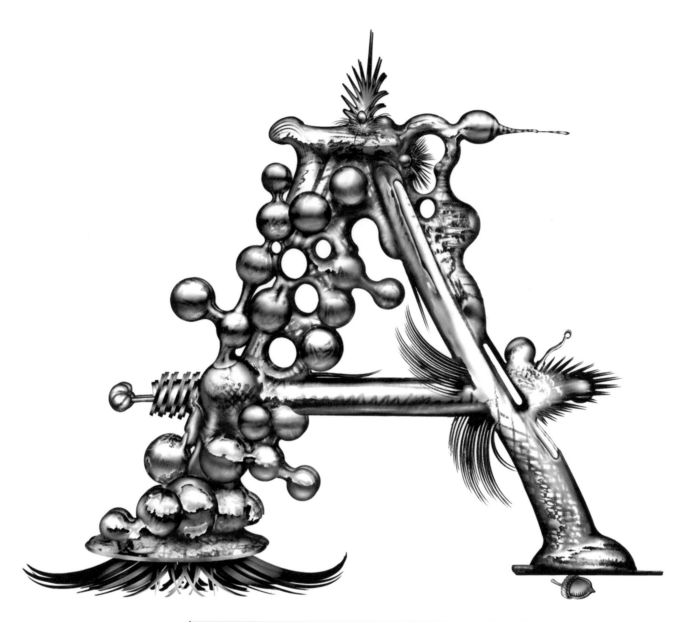

is for | **apperceptive achatina**

Apperceptive, *adj.* Conscious of its own consciousness; self-reflective with regard to *metaphysical* ends.

Achatina, *n.* A giant African snail.

Metaphysical, *adj.* Abstract; beyond nature or the physical; supernatural.

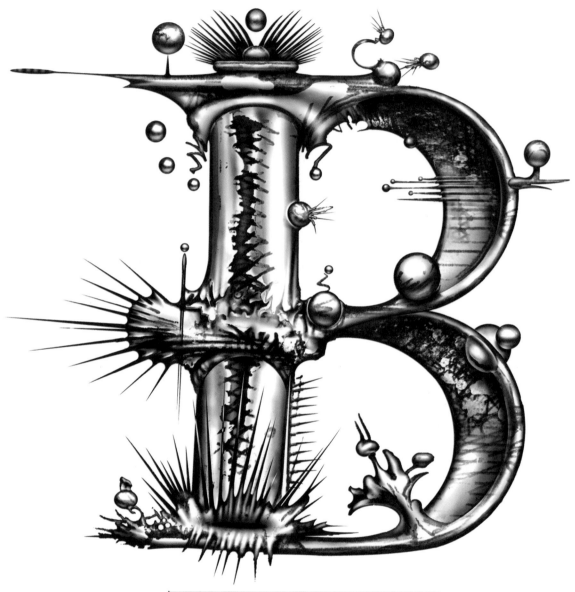

is for | **bifoliated bonito**

Bifoliate, *adj*. Having two leaves or leaflets.

Bonito, *n*. Any of several large fish of the mackerel family.

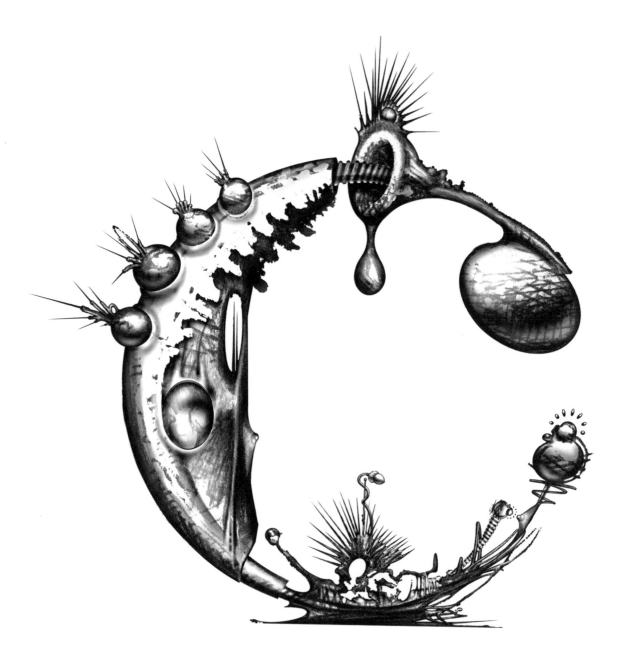

is for | caoutchoucoidal chelonia

Caoutchoucoidal (kow'chookoidal), *adj.* Made of India rubber, an elastic gum, or the dried juice of one of numerous tropical plants of the dogbane, spurge, and nettle families. Caoutchoucoidal objects are extremely elastic and impervious to water and to nearly all other fluids.

Chelonia (ki-lo-nie), *n.* Tortoises and turtles.

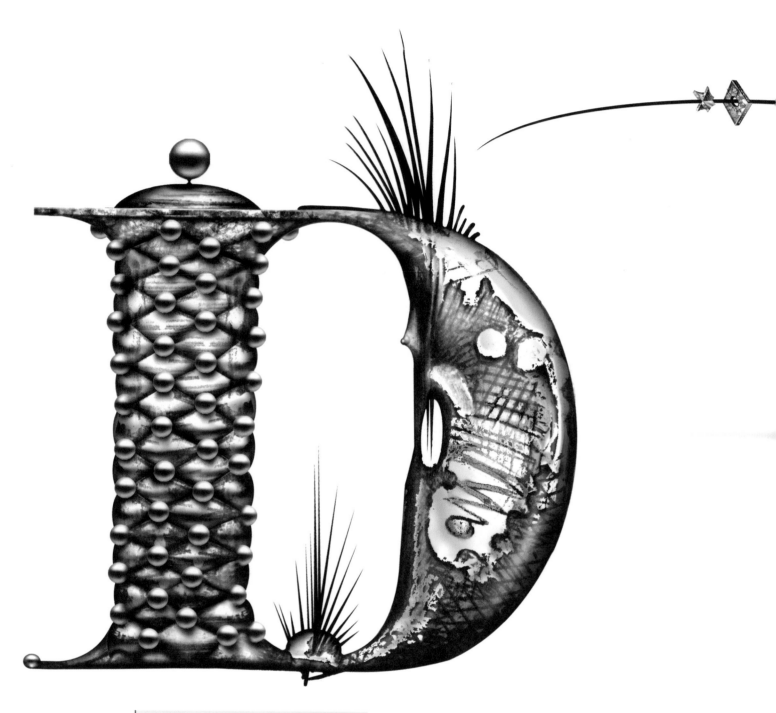

is for | **daedal doodle**

Daedal, *adj.* Cunningly or ingeniously formed; characterized by skillful workmanship.

Doodle, *vi.* Draw aimlessly.

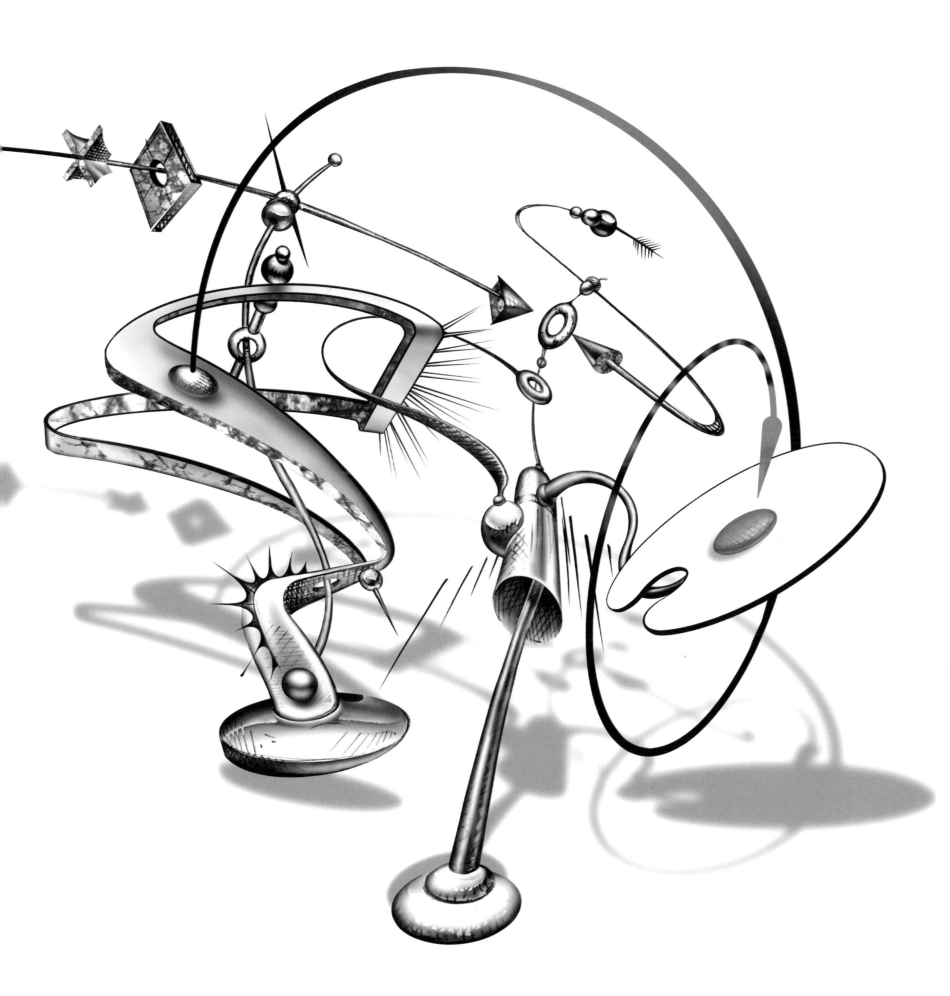

is for | **eohippus's epizoon**

Eohippus, *n.* The oldest known horse-like animal.

Epizoon, *n.* An animal that lives on the surface of another animal, whether parasitically or *commensally*.

Commensally, *adv.* Characterized by eating at the same table or living together for mutual benefit.

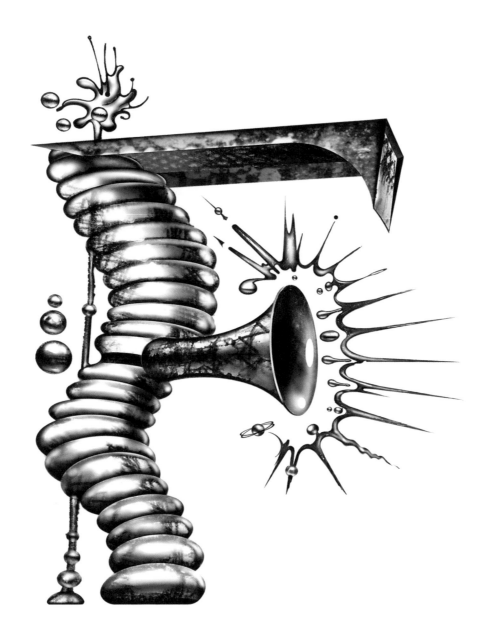

is for | **fanfare for feloid fig faun**

Fanfare, *n.* The sounding of trumpets.

For, *prep.* With reference to or in regard to.

Feloid, *adj.* Having the characteristics of the cat family.

Fig faun, *n.* A mythical creature, represented as living in desert places and eating figs.

is for | **ganoid gubbins**

Ganoid, *adj.* Of or pertaining to a subclass of fish covered with polished boney plates of scales.

Gubbins, *n.* A device, gizmo or gadget; something unspecified whose name is either forgotten or not known.

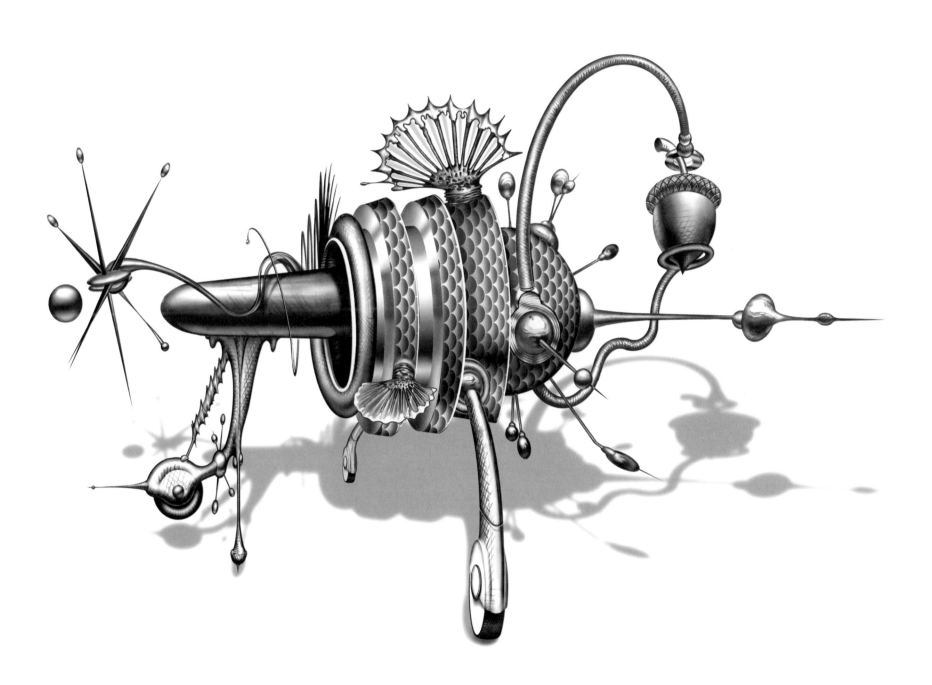

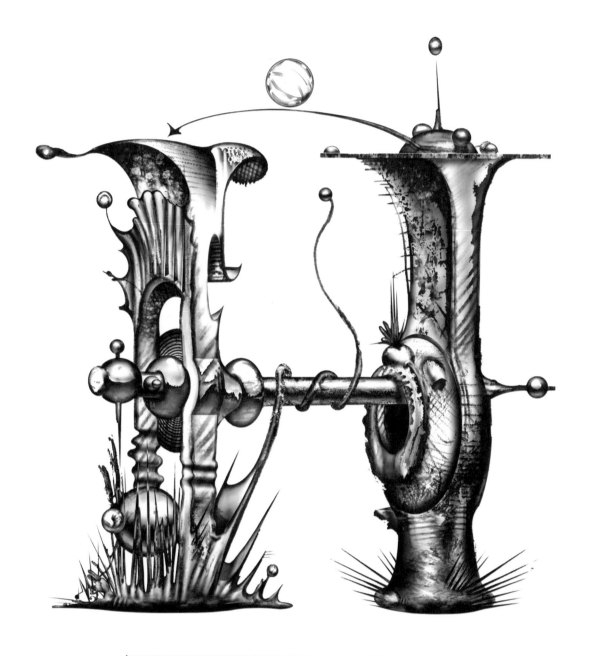

is for | hedonistic helix

Hedonistic, *adj.* Devoted to pleasure-seaking.

Helix, *n.* Any spiral, either lying in a single plane or, especially, moving around a cone, cylinder, etc. as the thread of a screw.

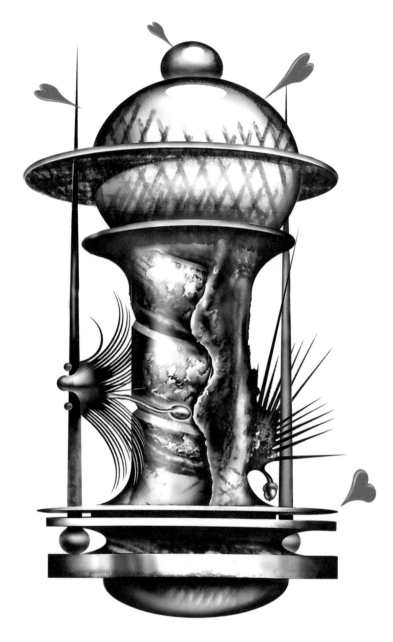

is for | **inamorato inamorata**

Inamorato, *n.* A man loved; a woman's lover.

Inamorata, *n.* A woman loved; a man's lover.

is for | **Jansky's jambalaya**

Jansky, Karl Guthe. 1905-50 engineer, a pioneer in radio astronomy.

Jansky, *n.* A unit of flux density fgor electromagnetic radiation, used cheifly in radio astronomy.

Jambalaya, *n.* A dish of Creole origin, consisting of rice cooked with ham, sausage, chicken, or shellfish, herbs, spices, and vegetables.

rice

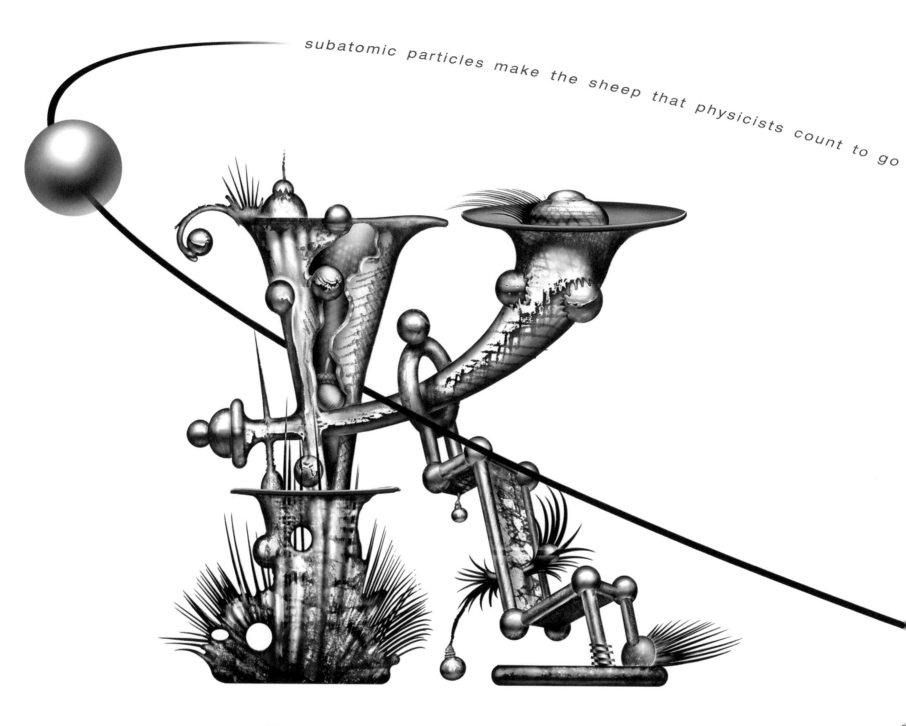

is for | **kaonic karakul**

Kaonic, *adj.* Pertaining to or composed of one of several types of subatomic particles of smaller mass than a proton.

Karakul, *n.* An asiatic breed of sheep.

to sleep

is for | **lissome logophile loach**

Lissome, *adj.* Lithe, nimble, flexible.

Logophile, *n.* A lover of words.

Loach, *n.* A small river fish of a family related to carp, having a long, narrow body and spines around it's mouth.

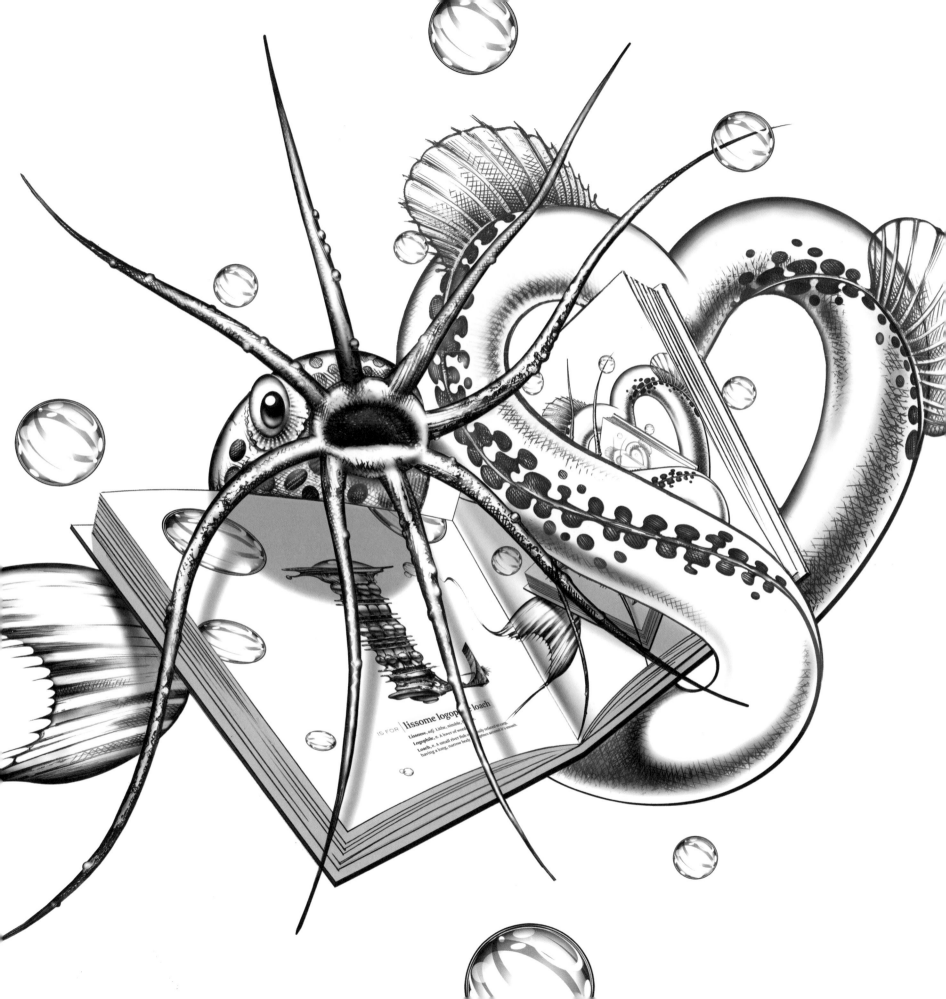

IS FOR | lissome logophile loach

Lissome, adj. Lithe, nimble, [...]
Logophile, n. A lover of words [...] only [...]
Loach, n. A small river fish [...] often around it's mouth,
having a long, narrow body [...]

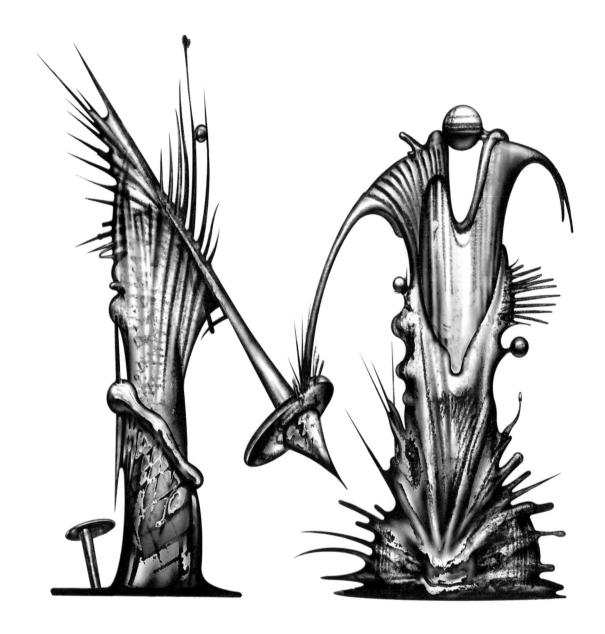

is for | microcephalic minotaur

Microcephalic, *adj.* Abnormally small-headed.

Minotaur, *n.* The bullheaded monster in the *Cretan Labyrinth*.

Cretan Labyrinth, *n.* A maze consisting of a single path winding back and forth to a center point in a series of seven concentric rings (google it). It was designed and constructed by the inventor Daedalus to confine the Minotaur.

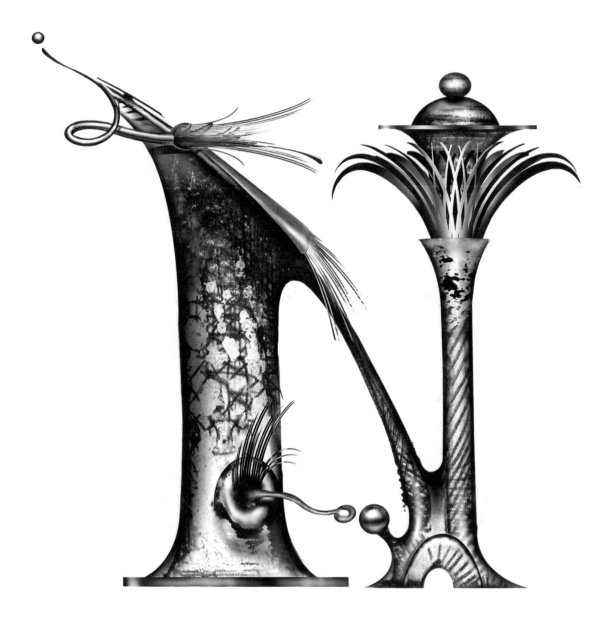

is for | **nidus naga's nucivorous nidicolous**

Nidus, *n.* A nest or breeding place: a place where anything is originated, harboured, developed, or fostered: a place of lodgement or deposit.

Naga, *n.* A snake, especially the cobra: a divine snake (Hindu myth).

Nucivorous, *adj.* Nut-bearing.

Nidicolous, *adj.* (Of young birds) staying long in the nest.

is for | **osmotic osprey**

Osmotic, *adj.* Pertaining to the tendency of a fluid, usually water, to pass through the semipermeable membrane into a solution where the solvent concentration is higher, thus equalizing concentrations of materials on either side of the membrane.

Osprey, *n.* A large, harmless hawk found worldwide that feeds on fish and builds a bulky nest often occupied for years (tell it to the fish).

swiss cheesesque artist rendering
of a semipermeable membrane

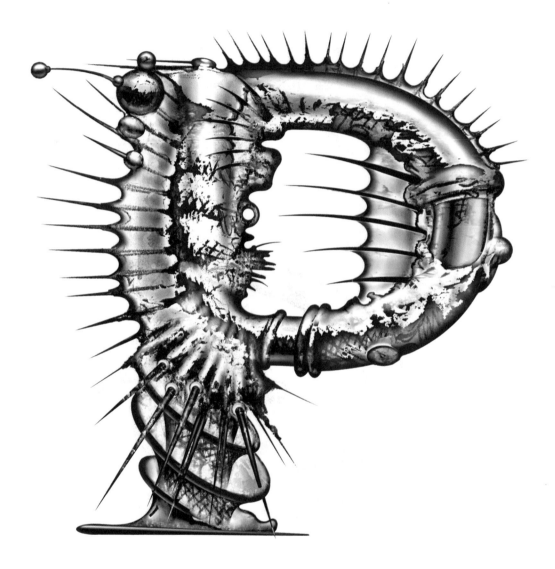

is for | **pangrammatic pappus**

Pangrammatic, *adj.* Pertaining to a sentence containing all the letters of the alphabet

Pappus, *n.* A ring or parachute of fine hair or down which grows above the seed and helps to disseminate composites and some other plants, e.g., dandelions, by means of wind.

is for | **quodlibetical quahog**

Quodlibetical, *adj.* Not confined to a particular subject; discussed at pleasure for curiosity or entertainment.

Quahog, *n.* A large species of clam.

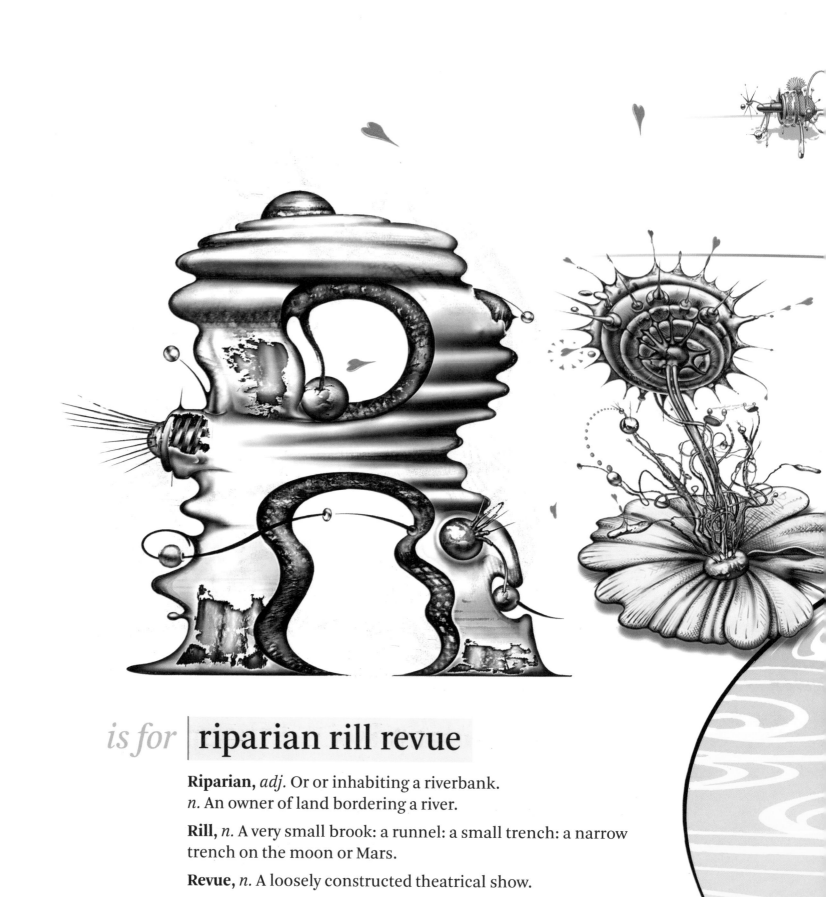

is for | **riparian rill revue**

Riparian, *adj.* Or or inhabiting a riverbank.
n. An owner of land bordering a river.

Rill, *n.* A very small brook: a runnel: a small trench: a narrow trench on the moon or Mars.

Revue, *n.* A loosely constructed theatrical show.

is for | seraphim's simulacrum

Seraphim, *n.* Members of the highest order of angels; persons of angelic character or appearance.

Simulacrum, *n.* An unreal or counterfeit resemblance.

is for | **tegulated tapir's transvolation**

Tegulated, *adj.* Composed of plates overlapping like tiles. [Latin tegula, n. A tile.]

Tapir, *n.* A large odd-toed *ungulate*, eating at night, with a long flexible proboscis. Several species are found in S. America, Malacca, etc.

Transvolation, *n.* The act of flying beyond ordinary limits.

Ungulate, *n.* A mammal having hoofs.

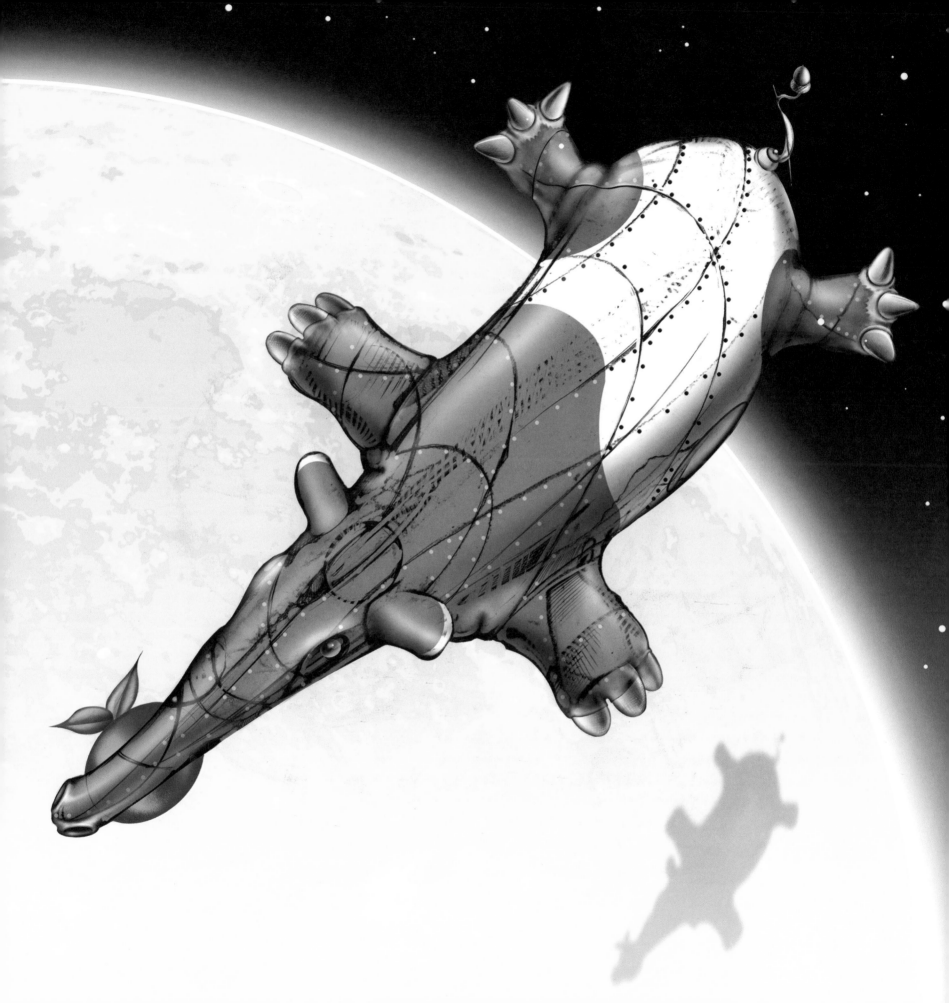

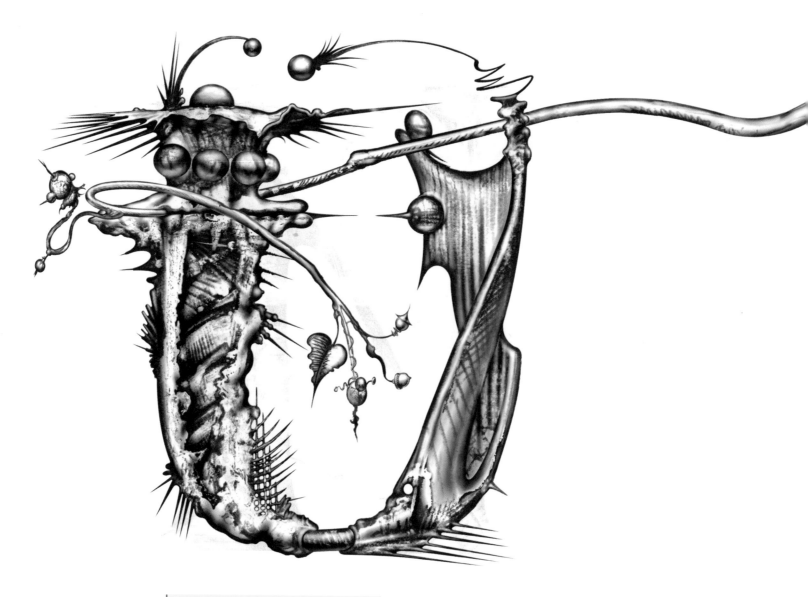

is for | **ursula urano**

Ursula, *n.* A beautiful North American butterfly. Its wings are nearly black with red and blue spots and blotches. Also called Red-spotted Purple.

Urano, *combining form.* Denoting the sky, the heavens, or the roof of the mouth.

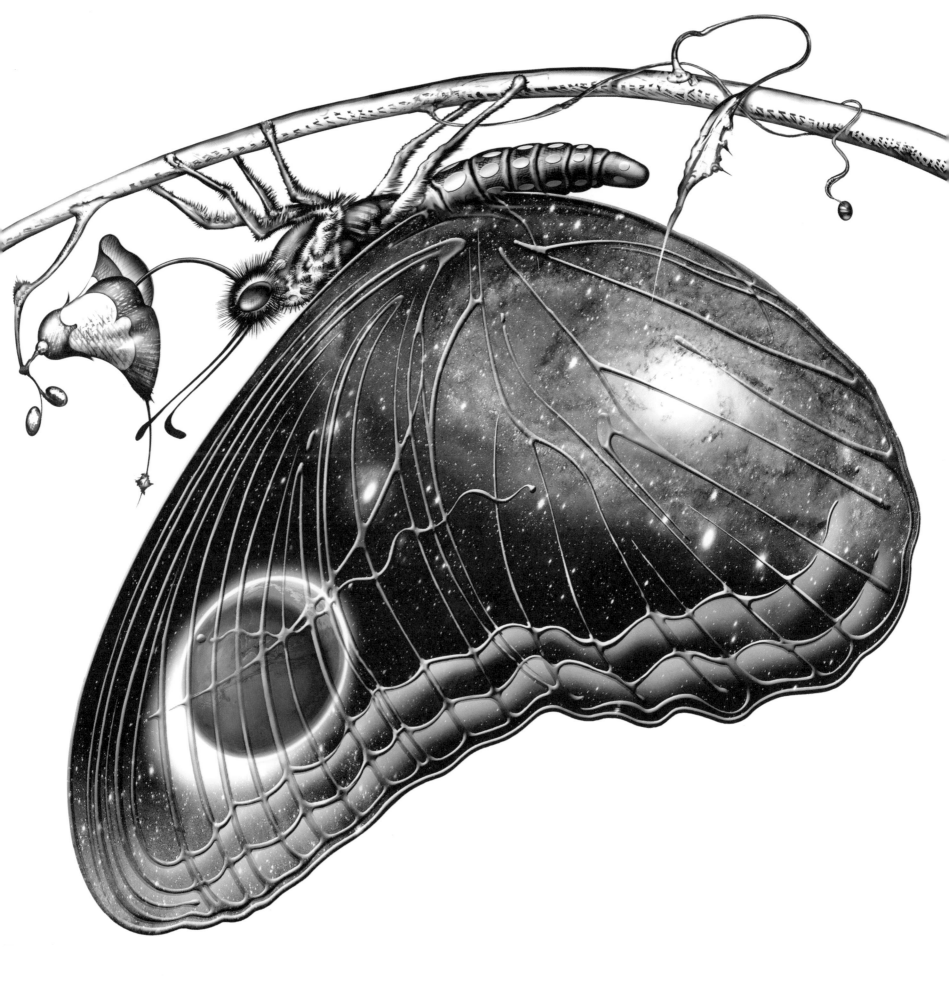

Verso, *n.* The left-hand page of an open book, the reverse of a coin or metal.

is for | **vedalia's vaccary voluted vade-mecum**

Vedalia, *n.* Australian ladybug.

Vaccary, *n.* A cow house.

Voluted, *adj.* Grooved or twisted in spirals.

Vade-mecum, *n.* [**Latin "go with me"**] A handbook or pocket-companion.

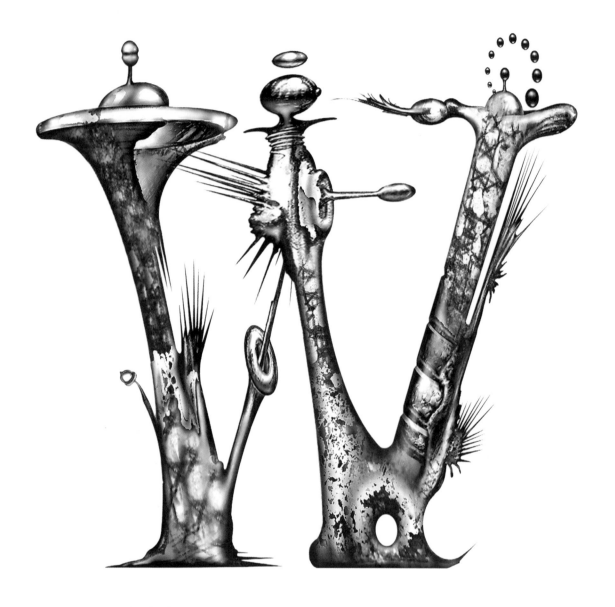

is for | **woubit's whigmaleerie**

Woubit, *n.* A hairy caterpillar.

Whigmaleerie, *n.* A trinket or knickknack; a fantastic ornamentation; a whim.

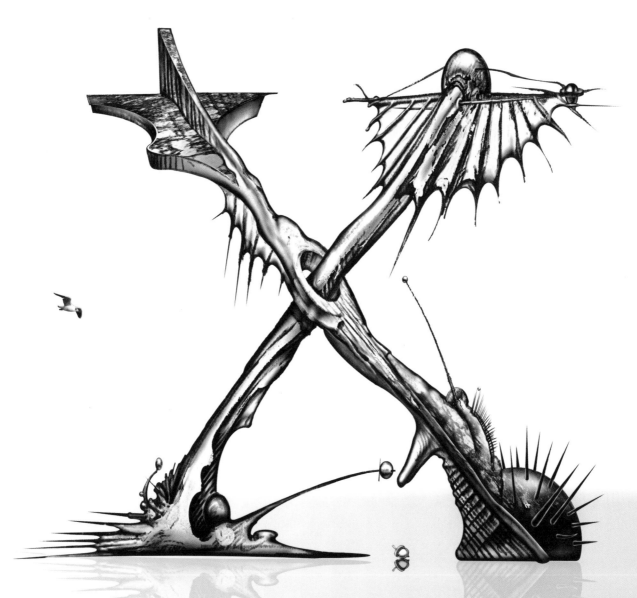

is for | xenomorphic xenobiosis xenium

Xenomorphic, *adj.* In geology, having a form that is not normal as a result of outside pressures. Said of the constituents of igneous rocks in which the outward form is irregular owing to contact with adjacent minerals.

Xenobiosis, *n.* A form of communal life in which two colonies of different species live together on friendly terms, but do not rear their young in common.

Xenium, *n.* A gift to a guest.

is for yava-skin ypsiliform ylem

Yava-skin, *n.* A kind of Elephantiasis caused by the habitual use of *Kava*.

Ypsiliform, *adj.* Y-shaped.

Ylem, *n.* In cosmology the original matter that existed before the formation of chemical elements, pre-Big Bang matter.

Kava, *n.* A Polynesian shrub, of the pepper family, the aromatic roots of which are used to make an intoxicating beverage.

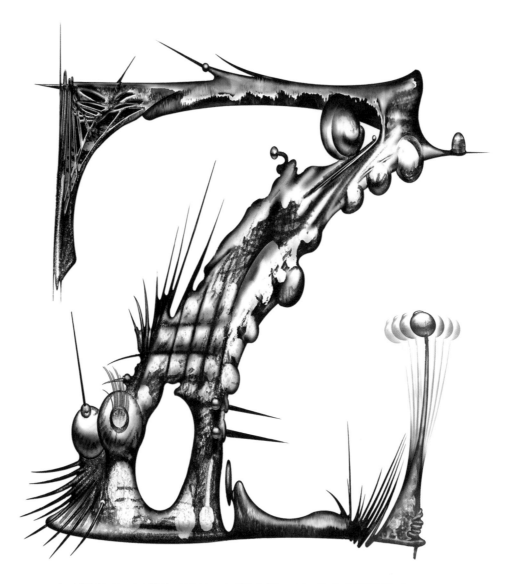

is for | **zooid zeppelin's zygote**

Zooid, *n.* An organic body or cell having locomotion, as a spermatic cell.

Zeppelin, *n.* A dirigible, cigar-shaped airship of the type designed by Count Zeppelin (c. 1900).

Zygote, *n.* The product of the union of two *gametes*; by extension, the individual developing from that product.

Gamete, *n.* A sexual reproduction cell; an egg cell or sperm cell.

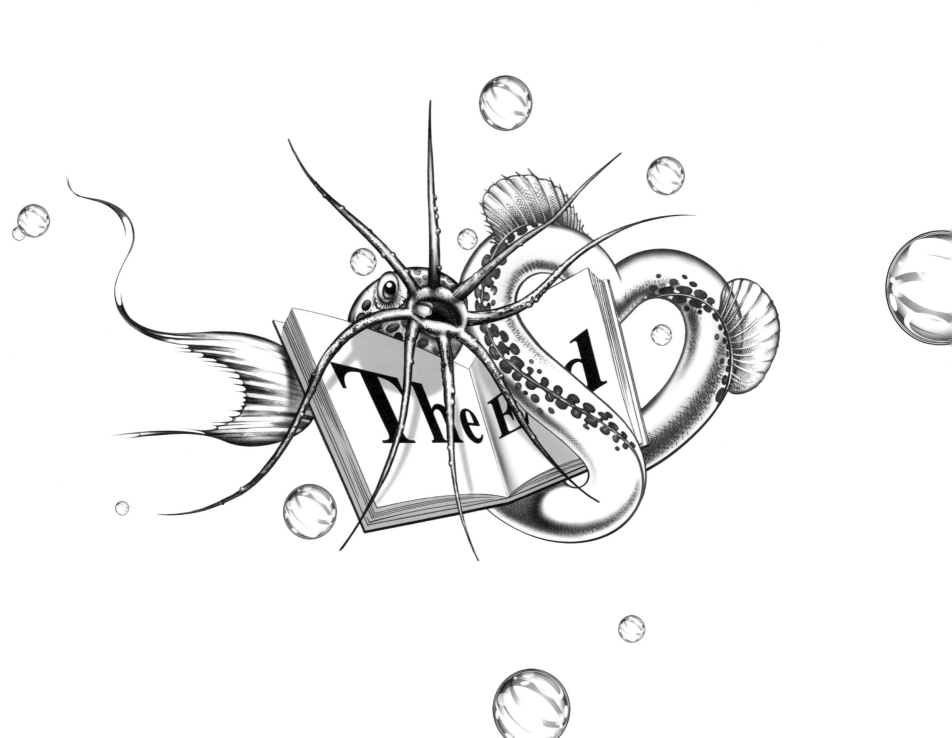